James Gra

The Man

Methuen Drama

Published by Methuen Drama 2010

1 3 5 7 9 10 8 6 4 2

Methuen Drama
A & C Black Publishers Limited
36 Soho Square
London W1D 3QY
www.methuendrama.com

Copyright © James Graham 2010

James Graham has asserted his rights under the
Copyright, Designs and Patents Act, 1988,
to be identified as the author of this work

ISBN 978 1 408 13216 6

A CIP catalogue record for this book is available from
the British Library

Typeset by MPS Limited, A Macmillan Company
Printed and bound in Great Britain by
CPI Cox & Wyman, Reading, Berkshire

Whippet Productions
in association with Neil McPherson for the Finborough Theatre
presents

THE MAN

by James Graham

FINBOROUGH | THEATRE

Productions

First performance at the Finborough Theatre, London: Tuesday, 25 May 2010
The Man was first performed as part of Vibrant - *A Festival of Finborough
Playwrights* at the Finborough Theatre on 17 October 2009.

The Man
by James Graham

Cast

The Man is performed by a rotating team of actors including

Ben	**Samuel Barnett**
	Leander Deeny
	James Graham
	George Rainsford
Inland Revenue	**Michelle Luther**
	Stephanie Thomas
	Lizzy Watts

The performance lasts approximately one hour.

There will be no interval.

Our patrons are respectfully reminded that, in this intimate theatre, any noise such as rustling programmes, talking or the ringing of mobile phones may distract the actors and your fellow audience-members.

Director	**Kate Wasserberg**
Designer	**Fly Davis**
Lighting Designer	**Tom White**
Production Photography	**Matt Humphrey**
Stage Manager	**Eleanor Randal**
Press	**Jenn Reynolds** for **Target Live**
Image Design	**Andreas Brooks**
Producers	**Caroline Dyott** and **Tara Wilkinson**

Samuel Barnett
Ben

Trained at the London Academy of Music and Dramatic Art.

Theatre includes *Women Beware Women* (National Theatre), *The Whisky Taster* (Bush Theatre), *When You Cure Me* (Bush Theatre), *Dealer's Choice* (Menier Chocolate Factory and West End), *The Marriage of Figaro* (Royal Exchange Theatre, Manchester), *The Accrington Pals* (Chichester Festival Theatre), *The History Boys* (National Theatre, International Tour and Broadway) for which he won a Drama Desk award for Best Performance for a Featured Actor in a Play, Newcomer of the Year and Best Supporting Actor at the *WhatsOnStage* Theatregoers Choice awards, and was nominated for an Olivier Award and a Tony Award. Television includes *Miss Marple, Beautiful People, Desperate Romantics, Crooked House, John Adams, The Inspector Lynley Mysteries, Coupling* and *Strange*. Film includes *Bright Star, The History Boys* and *Mrs Henderson Presents*.

Leander Deeny
Ben

At the Finborough Theatre, Leander appeared in T*he Representative* (2008) and *A Torture Comedy*, part of *Vibrant – A Festival of Finborough Playwrights* (2009).
Trained at the London Academy of Music and Dramatic Art.
Theatre includes *Dr Faustus* (Watford Palace), *Victory* (Arcola Theatre), *Corporate Rock* (Latitude), *How to Beat a Giant* (Unicorn Theatre), *The Merchant of Venice* (Shakespeare's Globe) and *The Seduction of Almighty God* (Riverside Studios and Birmingham Rep).
Film work includes *Atonement* and the forthcoming *Captain America*. His first book, *Hazel's Phantasmagoria*, was published by Quercus in 2008, and is available as a BBC audiobook.

Michelle Luther
Inland Revenue

Trained at the Royal Welsh College of Music and Drama. Theatre includes *Arden of Faversham, The Cherry Orchard, Night Must Fall, And What Now?, The Crucible, The Ballad of Megan Morgan* (all Clwyd Theatr Cymru), *Ker-Ching* (Redbridge Drama Centre), *Romeo and Juliet* (Royal Academy of Dramatic Art) and *Crossings* (Sgript Cymru). Television includes *Tracey Beaker – The Movie Of Me, Daniele Cable: Eye Witness, EastEnders* and *The Bench*.

George Rainsford
Ben

At the Finborough Theatre, George appeared in *Men Without Shadows* (2007).
Trained at the London Academy of Music and Dramatic Art.
Theatre includes *Days of Significance* (Royal Shakespeare Company Tour), *All's Well That Ends Well* (for which he was nominated for the Ian Charleson Award) and *Chatroom/Citizenship* (both National Theatre), *Miles to Go* (Latitude), *Polar Bear* (Birmingham Rep), *The Three Musketeers* (Bristol Old Vic) and *Guy Fawkes Night* (Old Vic). Television includes *Waking the Dead* and *Doctors*.
Film includes *Wild Target* and *Souvenirs*.

Stephanie Thomas
Inland Revenue

Theatre at the Finborough Theatre includes *I Wish to Die Singing* (2005), *The Beaver Coat* (2006), *The Representative* (2006) and *The Northerners* (2010).
Trained at the Webber Douglas Academy of Dramatic Art.
Theatre includes *Frost/Nixon* (Gielgud Theatre), *The Merchant of Venice* (Greenwich Playhouse), *Her Naked Skin* (National Theatre), *Only When I Laugh* (National Tour), *The Tempest* (York Theatre Royal), and a rehearsed reading of *Millicent Scowlworthy* (Donmar Warehouse). Voiceovers include *The Damned United*, *Silent Witness* and *Mamma Mia!*

Lizzy Watts
Inland Revenue

Theatre includes *My Balloon Beats Your Astronaut* (Tristan Bates Theatre), *Dr Faustus* (Watford Palace), *Eight* (Ringling Festival Museum, Florida), *The Exquisite Corpse* (Edinburgh Festival), *Artefacts* (Bush Theatre) and *The Grizzled Skipper* (Nuffield Theatre, Southampton).
Television includes *Midsomer Murders* and *Hidden*.
Film includes *Sprawlers* and *Footsteps*.
Radio includes *Mountain of Light*, *Matilda*, *Towards Zero*, *Ruminations Upon Mortality* and *Our Mutual Friend*.

James Graham Playwright/Ben
As Playwright-in-Residence at the Finborough Theatre since 2005, James's plays have included *Albert's Boy* (2005), *Eden's Empire* (2006, and winner of the Pearson Catherine Johnson Best Play Award), *Little Madam* (2007) and *Sons of York* (2008).
Other theatre includes *Tory Boyz* (Soho Theatre), *A History of Falling Things* (Clwyd Theatr Cymru), *The Whisky Taster* (Bush Theatre) and *Huck* (The Theatre, Chipping Norton, Southwark Playhouse and National Tour). For television, his original comedy-drama *Caught in a Trap* was ITV1's primetime Boxing Day drama in 2008. Radio includes *How You Feeling, Alf?* and *Albert's Boy* for BBC Radio 4.
Forthcoming projects include a new play for the National Youth Theatre this summer and for National Theatre New Connections next year. He is currently under commission to the Theatre Royal Plymouth, the UK Film Council, Channel 4, and the Bush Theatre.

Kate Wasserberg Director
At the Finborough Theatre, Kate was previously Associate Director where she directed *Sons of York* (2008) and *Little Madam* (2007), both by James Graham, and *The Representative* (2008), *I Wish to Die Singing* (2005) and *The New Morality* (2005).
Kate is New Plays Director at Clwyd Theatr Cymru where she has directed *Pieces* by Hywel John, *The Glass Menagerie* by Tennessee Williams and *A History of Falling Things* by James Graham. She was Artistic Director of the *Write to Rock* project and the Assistant Director on *Noises Off* and *Arden of Faversham*. Other directing includes *2007 Schools Festival* (Young Vic), *Switzerland* (HighTide Festival), *Doing Lines*, *Blue Velvet* (Edinburgh Festival), *The Studio* (National Tour)

and *The Firebird* (Exeter Phoenix).
As an Assistant Director Kate has
worked at the Barbican, the Abbey
Theatre Dublin, the Young Vic,
Shakespeare's Globe and the
Theatre Royal Bath.

Fly Davis Designer
Trained at the Royal Academy of
Dramatic Art in Technical Theatre
Arts and Stage Management and on
the Motley Theatre Design Course.
Recent credits include Associate
Designer to John Napier on
Disconnect (Royal Court Theatre
Upstairs and transfer to the Elephant
and Castle Shopping Centre), and
Design Assistant on *The Whisky
Taster* (Bush Theatre). As Set and
Costume Designer credits include
When the Lilac Blooms (Leicester
Square Theatre), *My 15 Minutes
Musical* (New Wimbledon Studio),
*Bloody Poetry, A Madman's
Confession* (White Bear Theatre) and
The Malleables (Arcola Theatre).
Forthcoming designs include *The
Great British Country Fete* (Bush
Theatre and North Wall Theatre,
Oxford, Ustinov Studio, Bath,
Tobacco Factory, Latitude Festival
and the Drum Theatre, Plymouth).
Fly has also worked as a Costume
and Design Assistant for the English
National Ballet at the London
Coliseum, Paines Plough at the
Shunt Vaults, Nabokov at the Village
Underground and Punchdrunk at the
BAC. She is Associate Designer to
the physical theatre company
Dumbshow, and is the Co-Artistic
Director of Catapulting Cocoon.

Tom White Lighting Designer
At the Finborough Theatre, Tom was
Lighting Designer on T*he
Representative* (2006), *Little Madam*
(2007), *Love Child* (2007), *Sons of
York* (2008) and *Weapons of
Happiness* (2008).
Trained at Middlesex University on
the Technical Theatre Arts course.
Theatre includes *Pieces, A History of*
Falling Things (Clwyd Theatr
Cymru), *Whipping It Up* (West End
and National Tour), *Up The Cafe De
Paris* (New Players Theatre), *Dry
Sigh* (The Place), *Madness in
Valencia* (Trafalgar Studios), *The
Glass Menagerie* (Clwyd Theatr
Cymru and Welsh National Tour),
Where's My Desi Soulmate (Theatre
Royal Stratford East and Tour), *Turf,
50 Ways To Leave Your Lover* (Bush
Theatre), *The Pink Bedroom*
(Courtyard Theatre), *Poofloose with
Stephen De Martin, 1 Poof and a
Piano* (Edinburgh Festival), *Game?*
(Theatre 503 and UK tour), *Hedda
Gabler* (Bulandra Theatre,
Bucharest), *Mozart's Back, Emily's
Kitchen* (Edinburgh Festival) *Hamlet,
Malvolio and His Masters* (Southwark
Playhouse), *Deir Yassan Day*
(Bloomsbury Theatre), *Yesterday
Was a Weird Day* (BAC), *Cargo*
(Northern School of Contemporary
Dance), *Catching Dust* (Teatro Della
Contraddizione, Milan), *Miss Julie,
Sotoba Komachi, The Damask Drum*
(Greenwich Playhouse), *Snapshots,
Maybe Baby* (Old Red Lion Theatre),
A Servant Of Two Masters (New End
Theatre). Opera includes *La Boheme*
(Longborough Festival Opera),
Simon Boccanegra, The Pearl Fishers
(Feria De Valladollid, Spain), *The
Marriage Of Figaro* (National Tour),
The Immortal Orchestra In Concert
(The Roundhouse) and *The
Crocodile* (Arcola Theatre).
Musical credits include *Stacey
Solomon's Homecoming Concert*
(Freemantle Media), *Dick
Whittington, Sleeping Beauty*
(Broadway Theatre, Barking), *Alyona*
(Theatre am Lend, Graz, Austria)
and *Shola Ama in Concert* (The
Roundhouse). Tom's work has been
seen in Egypt, Italy, Romania,
Austria, Spain and France. Tom's
other production role credits include
the BBC Electric Proms and the Paris
Autoshow 2008.

Whippet Productions Producer
Whippet Productions is a young
theatre production company whose
focus is to promote new writing.
Whippet presents plays that are
contemporary, meaningful,
provocative and engaging – a
theatre for today that lasts beyond
tomorrow. The aim is to give
exciting writers the opportunity to
have their work presented in full-
scale professional productions at
early stages in their career. Previous
productions include *Public Property*
by Sam Peter Jackson (Trafalgar
Studios), *Many Roads To Paradise*
by Stuart Permutt (Finborough
Theatre) and *Natural Selection* by
Paul Rigel Jenkins (Theatre 503).
Whippet Productions was founded by
Tara Wilkinson, Elizabeth Brown and
Tom Atkins in 2007.

FINBOROUGH | THEATRE

"One of the most stimulating venues in London, fielding a programme that is a bold mix of trenchant, politically thought-provoking new drama and shrewdly chosen revivals of neglected works from the past." *The Independent*

"A disproportionately valuable component of the London theatre ecology. Its programme combines new writing and revivals, in selections intelligent and audacious." *Financial Times*

"A blazing beacon of intelligent endeavour, nurturing new writers while finding and reviving neglected curiosities from home and abroad." *The Daily Telegraph*

"Few leading fringe theatres have walked off with so many awards or promoted such a rich variety of writers as the Finborough." *Plays International*

"The Finborough Theatre has developed a reputation out of all proportion to its tiny size. It has played its part in the careers of many remarkable playwrights, directors, and actors." *Financial Times*

Celebrating its 30th anniversary in 2010, the multi-award-winning Finborough Theatre – led by Artistic Director Neil McPherson – presents both plays and music theatre, concentrated exclusively on new writing and rediscoveries of neglected works from the 19th and 20th centuries. Behind the scenes, we continue to discover and develop a new generation of theatre makers – through our vibrant Literary Department, our hugely successful internship programme, our Resident Assistant Director Programme, and our partnership with the National Theatre Studio – the Leverhulme Bursary for Emerging Directors.

Founded in 1980, artists working at the theatre in the 1980s included Clive Barker, Rory Bremner, Nica Burns, Kathy Burke, Ken Campbell, Jane Horrocks and Claire Dowie. In the 1990s, the Finborough Theatre became particularly known for new writing including Naomi Wallace's first play *The War Boys*; Rachel Weisz in David Farr's *Neville Southall's Washbag*; four plays by Anthony Neilson including *Penetrator* and *The Censor*, both of which transferred to the Royal Court Theatre; and new plays by Tony Marchant, David Eldridge, Mark Ravenhill and Phil Willmott. New writing development included Mark Ravenhill's *Shopping and F***king* (Royal Court, West End and Broadway), Conor McPherson's *This Lime Tree Bower* (Bush Theatre) and Naomi Wallace's *Slaughter City* (Royal Shakespeare Company).

Since 2000, New British plays have included Laura Wade's London debut with her adaptation of W.H. Davies' *Young Emma*, commissioned for the Finborough Theatre; Simon Vinnicombe's *Year 10* which went on to play at BAC's *Time Out* Critics' Choice Season; James Graham's *Albert's Boy* with Victor Spinetti; Sarah Grochala's *S27*; Nigel Planer's *Death of Long Pig*; Stewart Permutt's *Many Roads to Paradise* with Miriam Karlin (which transferred to Jermyn Street Theatre); Joy Wilkinson's *Fair*, and Nicholas de Jongh's *Plague Over England*, both of which transferred to the West End. London premieres have included Jack Thorne's *Fanny and Faggot* which also transferred to the West End. Many of the Finborough Theatre's new plays have been published and are on sale from our website.

UK premieres of foreign plays have included Brad Fraser's *Wolfboy*; Lanford Wilson's *Sympathetic Magic*; Larry Kramer's *The Destiny of Me*; Tennessee Williams' *Something Cloudy, Something Clear*; Frank McGuinness' *Gates of Gold* with William Gaunt and the late John Bennett in his last stage role (which also transferred to the West End); the English premiere of Robert McLellan's Scots language classic, *Jamie the Saxt*; and Joe DiPietro's *F***king Men* which transferred to the West End and was nominated for a WhatsOnStage award for Best Off-West End Production.

Rediscoveries of neglected work have included the first London revivals of Rolf Hochhuth's *Soldiers* and *The Representative*; both parts of Keith Dewhurst's *Lark Rise to Candleford*; *The Women's War*, an evening of original suffragette plays; Etta Jenks with Clarke Peters and Daniela Nardini; *The Gigli Concert* with Niall Buggy and Paul McGann; Noël Coward's first play, *The Rat Trap*; Charles Wood's *Jingo* with Susannah Harker; and the sell-out production of Patrick Hamilton's *Hangover Square*.

Music Theatre has included the new (premieres from Grant Olding, Charles Miller, Michael John LaChuisa, Adam Guettel, Andrew Lippa, Adam Gwon, and Rodgers and Hammerstein) and the old (the acclaimed *Celebrating British Music Theatre* series, reviving forgotten British musicals).

Awards for the Finborough Theatre include the Empty Space Peter Brook Award's Dan Crawford Pub Theatre Award, supported by Nica Burns and the Cameron Mackintosh Foundation (2005 and 2008), and the Empty Space Peter Brook Mark Marvin Award (2004). It is the only theatre without public funding to be awarded the prestigious Pearson Playwriting Award bursary (2000, 2005, 2006, 2007, 2009 and 2010) as well as twice winning Pearson's Catherine Johnson Award for Best Play written by a bursary holder.

www.finboroughtheatre.co.uk

FINBOROUGH | THEATRE

118 Finborough Road, London SW10 9ED
admin@finboroughtheatre.co.uk
www.finboroughtheatre.co.uk

The Finborough Theatre has the support
of the Pearson Playwrights' Scheme.
Sponsored by Pearson PLC.

The Leverhulme Bursary for Emerging
Directors is a partnership between the
National Theatre Studio and the
Finborough Theatre, supported by The
Leverhulme Trust.

The Finborough Theatre is a member of
the Independent Theatre Council and
Musical Theatre Matters UK.

Online
Join us at Facebook, Twitter, MySpace and
YouTube.

Mailing
Email admin@finboroughtheatre.co.uk or
give your details to our Box Office staff to
join our free email list. If you would like to
be sent a free season leaflet every three
months, just include your postal address
and postcode.

Feedback
We welcome your comments, complaints
and suggestions. Write to Finborough
Theatre, 118 Finborough Road, London
SW10 9ED or email the Artistic Director at
neilmcpherson@finboroughtheatre.co.uk

Friends
The Finborough Theatre is a registered
charity. We receive no public funding and
rely solely on the support of our
audiences. Please do consider supporting
us by becoming a member of our Friends
of the Finborough Theatre scheme. There
are four categories of Friends, each
offering a wide range of benefits. Richard
Tauber Friends – Charles Lascelles. Lionel
Monckton Friends – Anonymous. Philip
and Christine Carne. William Terriss
Friends – Tom Erhardt. Leo and Janet
Liebster. Peter Lobl.

Smoking is not permitted in the
auditorium and the use of cameras
and recording equipment is strictly
prohibited.
In accordance with the requirements of
the Royal Borough of Kensington and
Chelsea:
1. The public may leave at the end of the
performance by all doors and such doors
must at that time be kept open.
2. All gangways, corridors, staircases and
external passageways intended for exit
shall be left entirely free from obstruction
whether permanent or temporary.
3. Persons shall not be permitted to stand
or sit in any of the gangways intercepting
the seating or to sit in
any of the other gangways.

The Finborough Theatre is licensed by the
Royal Borough of Kensington and Chelsea to
The Steam Industry, a registered charity and
a company limited by guarantee. Registered
in England no. 3448268. Registered Charity
no. 1071304. Registered Office: 118
Finborough Road, London SW10 9ED. The
Steam Industry is under the Artistic Direction
of Phil Willmott. www.philwillmott.co.uk

Characters

Ben
Inland Revenue

How the play works
As the audience enter, they are given a receipt at random that corresponds with the individual stories listed here in the text.

Following the opening exchange between **Ben** and the **Inland Revenue**, the actor playing **Ben** begins choosing receipts from the audience in a random order, performing the story that corresponds with that particular receipt. Consequently, no one show is ever the same.

As such, the *opening exchange* and the *final exchange* between **Ben** and the **Inland Revenue** are the only segments of the play whose position is guaranteed.

The exchanges between **Ben** and the **Inland Revenue** that are not related to specific receipts must be added in by the actor whenever he sees fit within the journey of the performance.

'Helpful' advice from the original performance
When *The Man* premiered at the Finborough Theatre, the actor(s) playing the **Inland Revenue** performed live as opposed to being a recorded voice. They sat within the audience – part of it, if slightly removed (i.e. to the side or to the back). This seemed to effectively contribute to the live, interactive feel of the 'event'.

As implied by the text, the **Inland Revenue** is more than a single character. There is 'Lisa', a woman with whom **Ben** speaks to most, but also in one segment a suggestion that the **Inland Revenue** changes person during one of **Ben**'s calls. As before, the original production placed a separate character in a different part of the audience. All of this is up for grabs.

The presence of the *Sainsbury's* receipts should help to combat the unpredictability of audience numbers in any given show (i.e. once the number of 'key story' receipts have been taken up, extraneous *Sainsbury's* receipts can be handed out to all additional audience members). At the opposite end of the spectrum, a smaller audience can be given more than one receipt.

It's easier than it looks. And more fun, too.

James Graham

Simon and Garfunkel's 'The Boxer' *plays as lights up on* **Ben**, *staring out, awkwardly holding a handful of tax forms. The song fades from intro music into the more tinny sound of 'on-hold' music, as* **Ben** *stands waiting for his call to be taken.*

The music cuts out.

Inland Revenue   Hello, HM Revenue and Customs, Lisa speaking.

Ben   Oh, no it's me again, I'm still on hold.

Inland Revenue   It's who sorry?

Ben   Ben.

Inland Revenue   You've been transferred through to Self Employment.

Ben   Oh God, sorry, you sounded like the last girl. Woman.

Inland Revenue   That's ok. How can I help?

Ben   My tax return, I can't do it.

Inland Revenue   Can I take your name please?

Ben   Ben Edwards, 8th of the 2nd 82, 54D Elmbourne Road, London SW17 1XT / United Kingdom.

Inland Revenue   Just your name is fine, actually.

Ben   Ben Edwards.

Inland Revenue   And what's your tax reference number?

Ben   I don't know, that's what I'm ringing to find out.

Inland Revenue   It should be on your Self Assessment form.

Ben   Well, erm, which one, I've got lots.

Inland Revenue   It should be on all of them, actually. Which one are you looking at now?

Ben   Uh. I dunno; white with green writing.

Inland Revenue   What number is it, the form?

Ben Where's that number?

Inland Revenue It should be just above your tax reference number.

Ben . . . right, but –

Inland Revenue You know there's a series of numbers at the top of the form?

Ben Yeah.

Inland Revenue Read a couple of them out to me.

Ben 0 – 8 – 4 – 5, 3 – 0 – 0 –

Inland Revenue That's sounds like the phone number you rang.

Ben The ph – . . . oh yeah.

Inland Revenue Is your National Insurance number there?

Ben Yeah.

Inland Revenue (*pause*) Can I have that then please?

Ben 0 – 8 – 8 – 9 –

Inland Revenue Sorry, it should start with two letters.

Ben You said you wanted the number.

Inland Revenue National Insurance numbers are made up of letters and numbers, so if you –

Ben No, I know, I wasn't being funny or – sorry, it's just I / can't stand these types of . . .

Inland Revenue If you read out the whole thing then please?

Ben Hold on, there's a number on the side, is that it?

Inland Revenue That'll be the form you're holding; what's that number?

Ben SA100-23F.

Inland Revenue   Right. OK. Well your unique reference number should be right at the top above your employer reference but below your National Insurance number.

Ben   Below the . . . (hold) . . . right, 919/01/XP3504.

(*Waits.*) Hello?

Inland Revenue   I'm just processing that now, sir.

Ben   Oh no sorry I thought you might have been cut off, I wasn't being rude.

Is it raining in Wrexham?

Inland Revenue   No. Is it raining in London?

Ben   No.

Why am I with the / Wrexham office – ?

Inland Revenue   OK, I've got your details up, Mr Edwards, how can I help?

Ben   I've got stuck on my Self Assessment form.

Inland Revenue   Oh. Nice and early. If you file online it doesn't have to be with us until the 31st of next January.

Ben   No I'm not doing it online, I'm doing the paper one.

Inland Revenue   We do recommend filing / online, Mr Edwards –

Ben   No I can't, I just can't, I'm not doing it online.

Inland Revenue   OK. So you're stuck; how far have you got, which question?

Ben   Question 1.

Inland Revenue   Que – . . . 'Name'?

Ben   No, on my form, the red page with 'Employment' at the top, it says to write down how much I earned from either my P45 or my P60.

Inland Revenue   Right.

Ben   Well. Which one? P45 or P60?

Inland Revenue   Whichever one you've got.

Ben   I've got both.

Inland Revenue   One must be out of date.

Ben   They've both got the same date on.

Inland Revenue   There must be a mistake.

Ben   Well you sent them to me. Do you see what I mean; do you see why I'm confused?

Inland Revenue   What are the amounts on each of them?

Ben   There aren't any.

Inland Revenue   There aren't any?

Ben   No, there are – . . . I haven't had any regular employed work.

Inland Revenue   Then you don't need to fill that in, just go straight to the self employment section, OK?

Ben   OK. And that's just the next page is it?

Inland Revenue   Yes. And that should all be fine, OK? Anything else I can help you with?

Ben   I don't think so.

Inland Revenue   All right, then. Well, you've been speaking / to Lisa, and –

Ben   Hold on, wait, don't go, I'm stuck again.

Inland Revenue   OK.

Ben   Question 1 on *this* page; business name. I don't have a business name.

Inland Revenue   You're self employed, correct?

Ben   Yes.

Inland Revenue   So you are your business, basically. You just have to write in your name.

Ben   Ben Edwards?

Inland Revenue Yes. That's the name of your business.

Ben Huh. My name is the name of a business.

Inland Revenue Yes.

Ben (*smiles*) That's pretty . . . (*stops smiling*) . . . scary.

Inland Revenue You'll be fine, I'm sure.

Ben . . . Yeah? I get so . . . nervous about these things. They. Erm. Upset me. A little bit. I'm not used to them.

Inland Revenue Some people do find them a little stressful.

Ben Do they? Other people?

Inland Revenue Yes, that's why we're here. To guide you through the form.

Ben To 'gui –' . . . OK.

Inland Revenue Oh, look at that. Huh. Outside. It's just started to rain . . .

Ben . . . has it?

Inland Revenue Yeah. Just a little bit. And I didn't bring my umbrella.

Ben Oh no.

Inland Revenue That's all right, I only have to run out to the car.

Ben What car do you drive?

Inland Revenue Just a little Peugeot 206.

Ben What colour?

Inland Revenue Blue.

Ben What engine?

Inland Revenue Ooh crikey, now you're asking. Er, 13 . . . 1360? I think. CC. Or something.

Ben   Right.

Inland Revenue   How about you?

Ben   Oh no, I don't drive, don't know anything about cars.

Inland Revenue   Oh OK.

Ben   Can't make out anything you just told me, actually. 'Cept maybe blue.

Inland Revenue (*laughs*)   Right.

Ben (*laughs*)   Huh.

Inland Revenue   OK. Well do contact us again with any other queries –

Ben   Will I come back to you?

Inland Revenue   Not necessarily, there are quite a lot of us.

Ben Can I . . . sorry, if this is – if this sounds . . . erm, but can, can I ask for you? Maybe. Or –

Inland Revenue   Erm. Yes, if . . . if you like.

Ben   What do I say, just Lisa? 'Is Lisa there please?'

Inland Revenue   I can give you a reference number if you like. Just give that to the first one who answers and if I'm working, they'll transfer you through.

Ben   Are you sure?

Inland Revenue   Yeah, course. Any little problem you might have, just call.

Ben   . . . You might regret that.

Ben *steps out of his spot.*

A desk, covered in forms. Shoe boxes and shopping bags of receipts everywhere.

An empty box which says 'Expenses'; another which says 'Not Expenses'.

Ben This is a test.

I'm, erm . . . I'm not sure how it, it's going to, erm, work, but it's an idea, from this guy I'm seeing – not *seeing* 'seeing' like that kind of seeing, I just mean 'seeing', seeing, as in someone that I see, to talk to. Well not talk, really, because *he* doesn't say anything, he just sits there and listens to me, four till five, every second Friday.

But some other people have said they think it's a good way to do it. Not only to complete the actual, erm . . . form. (*Shiver.*) The form. But also as a, like a 'useful opportunity' to uh . . . well go through some of the . . . some of the other, erm, things. That have been, erm . . . going on. Kind of thing. If that . . .

I just . . . huh, honestly, sometimes, I don't know how I literally get through each day. Something takes over. A nervous, heart-racing, erm . . . 'ness'. And I just surrender to it.

I find a lot of things . . . 'difficult'. I feel like I'm behind on a lot of things, grown-up adult things, and I'm . . . and it's like I'm trying to catch up.

And, yes, forms are particularly bad, I just have no confidence, and the only thing forms really need is confidence, it just needs you to erm . . . to commit. Commit to knowing something. You know on *Who Wants to be a Millionaire* when the contestants always say, 'well it's different when you're actually sat in the chair, instead of just watching at home, you start to doubt everything you've ever known'. Well. That's a bit like what minute-to-minute, hour-to-hour life is like for me. A lot of the time.

This is my first tax return.

I've been pretending I don't have to do one and all year I've just been throwing my receipts, everything, into, into these shoe boxes and shopping bags and just kind of assuming it would all work out. Like maybe some little Inland Revenue elves would turn up in the night, like tooth fairies, and start filing everything. All the while chanting, 'tax doesn't have to be taxing. Tax doesn't have to be ta–...'

But they haven't. And so now I have to do it.

Some people have said 'take it to an accountant', but, urgh, just the idea of handing all my receipts over, to someone I don't know, them rifling through ... I couldn't, that's ... no, I couldn't. It would be like ... standing there naked and having a ... no. Couldn't.

They're a record of what we buy. Aren't they? And what we buy says, you know, a lot about, you know ... Who We Are. Especially now, in this day and ...

About what we *need*. Erm. Value. How much we're willing to pay for something.

And how often. And ...

So, yes, it's an absolute mess, yes. And I have literally no idea what you can put in as a business expense and what you can't. Literally not a clue. So every single time I exchanged money for something else, there's a record of it here. The ones you're holding are barely the tip of the ... death-hell. Erm. So let's ... shall we ...

Picks a member of the audience.

What have you got? What's your receipt for? Thank you ...

Sainsbury's receipt – any date

Ben   Oh, this is from the Sainsbury's on Balham High Road – do you know it?

I can finally walk in there with my head held high – well, not high, just, you know, at the ... normal gradient. But in those early months, when I first quit my proper job, and became, uh, 'self employed', I didn't have – oh God – I didn't have any money. It was before my granddad's inheritance came through.

So shopping, those first few months in Sainsbury's, I'd have rehearsed my, erm, my 'indignation' routine, at my card not going through. Just in case. 'What? Urgh, that bank, I can't believe they've done it again, they said they'd activated the card, grrr, I'm so cross. With them.' Kind of thing. You know, pretend I was off to withdraw some cash instead, ranting about how, how the banking system needed to pull its socks up, or something, and then, and just, never go back.

The irony of not having enough money on my Oyster Card to travel into town to meet a client to earn money to put on my Oyster Card was not lost on me. I'd have to call up Mum, or Dad, ask them to top it up for me online. Which really hampered my 'I'm absolutely fine, I know what I'm doing, Dad', argument.

Hated having to borrow money from them continually. My mum and dad aren't exactly . . . well, think of some rich mums and dads; they're not them. But they worried about me. On my own, down here. Obviously. Given my complete . . . erm . . . well, given what I was like. When I was growing up.

Steps into his 'Inland Revenue' spot again.

Inland Revenue   It can only be expenses directly related to the running of your business.

Ben   Oh. OK. Yeah. But I don't know what that means. Like these Sainsbury's receipts.

Inland Revenue   Is it for stationery or postage stamps or anything like that?

Ben   No, it's for broccoli and some hummus.

Inland Revenue   Then you can't claim it as expenses I'm afraid, as it didn't contribute to the success of your business.

Ben   It kept me alive. Isn't being alive directly contributing to the success of my business?

Inland Revenue   I'm afraid not, no. Not technically.

Ben Not technically?

Inland Revenue No.

Ben So no food.

Inland Revenue Try to think of it as being like . . . well, you know in your previous jobs?

Ben Yeah.

Inland Revenue You didn't have to pay for the phone calls yourself, or for printing anything out or posting anything, did you, the company did that.

Ben Yeah.

Inland Revenue Well, you have to pay for all of that yourself, now, don't you; so this is just collecting all those receipts together, adding up what are business expenses, and then taking them off the total amount you earned. So say if you earned twenty thousand, but two thousand of that was spent on your business, we'll only tax you on eighteen.

Ben Right. OK. Erm. Right, yeah OK, cool, thank you.

Steps out of his spot.

Does anyone have any other food ones, Sainsbury's, then or . . . ? (*Begins collecting the receipts up.*) Sorry. That was a waste of time, giving you those. Thank you.

Beer can drinking hat – 13 August 2009

Ben Oh, this was a birthday present for Josh. One of those – have you seen them, like Homer Simpson hats, a beer can either side, and straws that . . . it was a joke, him being too stiff sometimes to actually pick up a can, or a pint of . . .

I can joke about it, see. Being the twin. It's sort of allowed.

Actually, though, one of the amazing things about us – not amazing, sorry, 'we're amazing', I didn't mean it like that, but the . . . *interesting*, the interesting thing about me and

Josh – erm, Josh and I (sorry. Horrendous, today), is that I was born on a day all to myself, and so was he. Despite being twins.

You do hear it happening now and again, sometimes in extreme cases, when labour spans midnight, kind of thing. There's this case happening now about . . . I think it's the Conway twins, born either side of the September 1st cut off point for the academic year, and the local school is saying the older twin has to start in one year, and the younger one has to wait to start the next – I know. Mad. There have been twins born in different years technically, either side of New Year's Eve. And, for that reason, the Hegenberger twins have a whole millennium separating them. So . . .

We're not *that*, erm, interesting. But essentially Josh was born at 11.56pm on the 7th of February, which in 1982 was a Monday, and I was born at 12.04. Which was a Tuesday. So that's only eight minutes separating us. But one whole day. (*Beat. Thinks. Goes to say something. Doesn't. Beat . . .*)

OK. Erm . . .

Right, OK, erm, so this thing with Josh . . .

So they thought something was wrong with both of us, actually, as soon as we were born. They only had to look at our toes. Both our big toes bend in towards the little toes; I won't show you; hate it. I never get my feet out. Ever. Swimming. In the flat. Ever.

But it took Josh's first accident for the doctors to work out it was FOP.

FOP stands for Fibrodysplasia Ossific Progressiva. Which is really hard to say if you've never said it before but I've said it about a hundred thousand times. So.

It basically means that bone grows where it shouldn't. When a normal person bruises themselves or breaks a bone, the bone repairs itself. Yeah? With FOP people, extra bone grows into the damaged area. So, like, for example if an FOP person fell into a wall and broke his or her arm, the muscle there, as it's repairing, might actually be replaced with bone. And it's very hard to stop this from happening and there's no cure and so over the course of your life you eventually grow something akin to a second skeleton. Which can make it really difficult for you to move and in some cases breathe.

I think Josh first got taken to hospital when he was about one and a half after cracking his elbow against the kitchen table leg – I don't remember any of this, obviously. And that's when they found out we had it. Well that's when they found out Josh had it. I hadn't had any accidents so I hadn't developed any extra bone yet.

There's, erm . . . huh, there's this famous church with a crooked spire in Chesterfield. We hadn't always lived there, moved around a bit, born in Guildford actually, hence the slight odd (*points to his mouth*). But I remember Granddad once making a joke about Josh, when he was looking a little stiff as he got older, being like that crooked Chesterfield spire. It Did Not Go Down Well with my mum.

But he was so, so, so much braver than I was. Josh. As kids. He was so determined that it wouldn't stop him doing things. Mum would . . . she'd never let us go out and play in the street or do sports or anything. At first. FOP sufferers aren't meant to run. They're not meant to jump. Or ride bikes. Slide down the banister. Or do a lot of things. Basically. Me, I was fine with that, some of the things sounded so . . .

Huh, there was this, erm – just to prove how we were so . . . how Josh was more . . . erm, this one time when he borrowed Darren Butler's bike from next door, we were about six, seven. I was in the garden with my mum, the gate was closed but Josh was on the other side, in the street, for some reason. It was a Saturday, which meant Dad was at Homebase. I don't know why; but that's what Dads do on

Saturday. I guess I kind of assumed that when I grew up to become a man, that you would find out, that reasons would 'present' themselves to go to Homebase and Halfords on a Saturday morning. But they haven't yet.

Anyway, I saw Darren gives Josh his bike – I think Josh had given him some . . . I dunno, football cards or something, I couldn't really see. His bike still had stabilisers on so Josh could get on it fine and he just took off down the street, wobbling a lot. And Mum turned and saw.

You know the worst feeling in the world is when your mum or dad momentarily stop being grown-ups. The sound of my mum screaming, that kind of scream where they've already started to cry, and it . . . was like she'd been stabbed, or something.

We lived on a cul de sac and so it wasn't a long street, but she still couldn't catch him as he went round the bottom of the road and came back towards our house.

I just stood and watched. Crying. On the other side of the closed gate.

Thought he was going to be in *so* much trouble. But one of the plus points about FOP is that your parents never smacked you.

He was a massive Michael Jackson fan. I didn't get it myself, At All, but Josh was *obsessed*. He'd try all the moves. Which he wasn't supposed to, obviously, but he'd show me the things he was working on, as I sat on my bed. That twist and kick with the leg. The moonwalk, naturally. Accidents happened. As they do. He kicked our desk with his foot, fracturing his ankle. Banged his shoulder against our wardrobe. And the flare ups started to happen – that's what they're called. Flare ups. And it would get harder and harder for him to moonwalk, because he was growing this extra bone, but he'd keep going. Showing off in the playground.

I think it was in the last year of primary school that Dean Rogers accidentally kicked me in the wrist. He was meant to kick the bag of rubbish I was taking out of the dining hall; it was my turn. Rota, thing. Dean always did that to the person taking the rubbish out but despite years of practice he was still bafflingly imprecise, and his boot connected with my wrist instead, and it hurt, really hurt, so I fainted.

'Caterpillar'. 'Boots for an angry generation'.

Anyway, that's when they found out. I was fine. I was absolutely fine. Not one extra bit of bone grew. It just healed. Perfectly.

I didn't have it.

But my toe? I know. No one could explain it. Doctors joked that it was a 'sympathy toe'. Growing up together in the womb. Or something.

Worse thing is, though, it didn't matter. Really. I didn't change, I didn't want to do any of those things, still. Run. Jump. Roll. Ride anything I was happy just . . . opting out of it all.

But anyway, so yes, the beer can hat was a present for Josh. Don't think that's really an expense, do you?

Return train ticket Balham to Peckham Rye – 17 May 2009

Ben   Peckham, right, well all these train tickets to Peckham, if there are any more, these are just . . . that's where Rachel lived. Lives, still. I assume.

In fact, May, God, well, yeah, this would be the last time I, erm . . . I went over to see her. Things had been a little . . . 'off', for a bit. A while. This was kind of a 'summit' meeting. I don't think I knew what was going to come out of my mouth. What it was I wanted. Still.

She'd always been about three divisions out of my league. Like she was Premiership, and I was Vauxhall Conference.

Or whatever they call it now. Stupidly pretty, this amazing blonde hair, in like a bob – is that what's . . . ? (*Demonstrates.*) And she was a dancer, well, dance choreographer. So. You know.

I'd left my job at the council and been trying to get the website thing going, so I was really all over the place. But then again *she*, she was the one who was out, working at that fucking Hoxton bar place (sorry, swearing, just showing off), at this bar in the evenings and I Hated going there. All the guys she worked with looked like they'd stepped out of GQ magazine, and they all looked at me with amazement that . . . that she was . . . you know, asking, like, 'why?' I don't know, ask her, if it's so . . .

Maybe there's only so many times you can be asked that before you start . . .

We went to the White Horse. This time. Didn't want to go to her house, better if it was neutral ground. If we decided to stay together, then I'd be going back to hers, of course, but . . .

She'd been crying a bit, so she was wearing sunglasses but I remember it feeling like the first really proper day of spring, first hot one anyway so it didn't look odd.

She'd given up trying by that point, I think. And we were just there to . . . finalise.

It's so idiotic really. That it was me leaving *her*. I'm sure she realises that now.

It's just it had been, it'd been, like, three years, and I know that's hardly a lifetime, but at . . . I suppose I started to realise at this age, at our age, after that long with someone, you're meant to . . . aren't you? Do something 'more'. Grow up, I suppose. But I . . . . I didn't – it didn't feel. Right. Erm. Because I suppose that literally really is becoming a grown-up, isn't it? Saying bye to being young, to being . . . saying bye to the future being possibly *anything*. And instead saying, no, it's going to be specifically *this*. Forever.

You have little bits of it creeping in during your twenties. Breaking you in to the idea of 'manhood'. Huh. Twenty-five I remember was pretty tough; handing your Young Person's Railcard back – 'oh, you want it back, oh OK, why sorry? Oh I see, I'm not young anymore'. Twenty-five? Jesus. That's when you leap up a block on questionnaires, too; now I tick the '25 to 34' box – 'really, you're not differentiating between me and a thirty-four-year old? OK. Fine.'

The '25 and over' category in The X Factor. That one where they all say 'but it's my last chance!'

Twenty-five.

(*Looks at the ticket.*) Oh. God, hmm. I'd, uh . . . I'd bought a day *return*.

Maybe I had known what was going to come out of my mouth after all.

Computer / web cam / software, John Lewis – 21 March 2009

Ben   Oh, yeah, this . . . oh God, my new computer and stuff. Oh well this can definitely go in. Can't it? Yeah?

I was so stressed. Computers, it's like the form thing again. You have to commit, when you're clicking on something, saying yes to something, saying cancel to something, and I just don't . . . 'function'. Like that. So . . .

But I needed a computer and I needed a web cam and I needed a lot of other things for my business. For the thing I was going to do. Luckily – I bought him lunch and a pint afterwards – luckily Neil was in town that day, my web designer, and he agreed to go with me to John Lewis, because basically if any of the sales staff approached me I'd buy the thing I was standing next to at the time and probably a fridge freezer and anything else they offered me because I'm just rubbish at that.

Maybe I should tell you what I . . .

OK. Yeah. Basically my business is this. I teach. Give seminars. Online. I post videos, which I record, of me teaching. There you go.

Anything from, uh, history, quite a bit. English Literature. For GCSE, I'm talking. And A Levels. For students to watch online. And anyone, really. See what you do is subscribe, only a tiny little amount, each month, and then you get access to any of my videos – I'd show you some if I had . . . and I also do these online forums where you can (what do you call it) just type in with your questions, live, and then I answer them live, kind of thing.

And I know what you're thinking. That I am probably the worst person to be doing something like this. Possibly some of you are parents and are thinking, 'really? This guy, in my living room? Speaking to my children? Hmm'.

But oddly enough, for whatever reason . . . I think it's because I care so much.

I gave an example to everyone, all my friends, and Josh and Mum and Dad, and people, Aunty Sue (random); a five minute summary of the French Revolution. And they all said it was . . . well really good. And that's when I came up with the idea.

It's at least putting to use the PGCE I studied for but was completely wasting.

(*Dropping the receipt into the 'Expenses' box.*)

Hooray! A proper definite real life expense! We should have a bell we can ring or something. When we get one. Or not, whatever.

iTunes receipts

The first time an iTunes receipt is picked out from the audience, begin with this opening introduction. Then continue as per when the specific music downloads are chosen.

Ben   OK, iTunes. Erm, well one of the ways I thought about getting through this is to play the songs I bought. Then it makes it feel more like I'm just kicking back, on my bed, listening to some music, instead of, erm . . . calculating what I owe the British government. So.

Black Beauty theme tune

Ben   Uh, just so you know, right, this was for work, not pleasure. Or some . . . weird, sex game. This was, like, a one-off video where I taught people how to play chess. And this was the knight. Obviously. Because it's a horse. A black horse, sometimes. And Black Beauty was a black horse. Hence the . . . song . . .

I could listen to this literally all day; it makes me so happy.

Might get it as a ringtone – actually, no, that'd ruin it.

Philip Glass – 'Metamorphosis Two'

Ben   Uh, yeah, this is Philip Glass. This one was just for me. Actually.

Dave Willets – 'I Am What I Am'

Ben   Um, yeah, teaching chess online. This is the soundtrack I used for the . . . Queen. Which I only realised after might be slightly . . . derogatory but I just thought it fitted, you know. She just, she flounces round the board, can go literally anywhere.

Well. I thought it was funny.

12 Viennettas, Iceland – 8 July 2009

Ben   12 Viennettas? Oh Christ, I know what this is. God, I'm not sure I even want to tell you. Do I? No.

OK, I will. Basically this is Chris, housemate. Well, lodger. Housemate implies . . . well, 'mate'. Actually, that's unfair, we do get on. Kind of. He's very particular about certain things, not because he's OCD, because I don't think he is – although, if we have time, I'll tell you about his 'toast plate' (man alive); like a separate plate upon which to do the buttering, before you transfer it to . . . anyway. Maybe it's because he's an actor. Sort of. In the sense that he was once 'cut' from an episode of Doctors four years ago, but still got paid, so has an agent, and so is an actor, technically, though what he actually does at the moment is a lot of temping.

I found him on Gumtree. Well, he found me on Gumtree. When I had to move down to Balham; Balham-slash-Tooting.

I really miss my old house. It was so lush.

I can't really believe I just said 'lush', but oh well.

A good 'tax-related' fact for you, here, about Cavendish Road, where I used to live; an interesting anomaly. It runs – no one knows it, do they?

It runs up from Balham towards Clapham Common. Well, it's one of the only streets in the country (I think – don't contradict me if not, there isn't time) where one end of the street is in one council's jurisdiction; and one end another. So the north end, that half of the street, is in Lambeth; the other half in Wandsworth. I know. Two halves of, like, the same whole. But different.

So one side of the same street have different refuse collection, on a different day, different people mending lampposts, etcetera.

The real kick in the teeth though is that Wandsworth Borough Council – who I used to work for, Education department, office slave, that was the job I quit – they have the cheapest council tax in the country. And Lambeth . . . uh, well, they don't.

I was on the Wandsworth side, I'm pleased to say. I'd taunt my neighbours by just . . . well . . . by doing nothing at all, actually, if I'm honest.

So, sorry. Chris. Living with me. Viennetta. Yes. Basically, one
summer, if we can call last year's summer a summer, he got a
promotions job handing out samples of Viennetta in the
street – crappy job in and of itself, but made doubly worse by
the fact that you have to store the Viennetta at home yourself.
Why? I don't know; in case of some sampling emergency and
you had to have a piece to hand, when you're bleeped, or
something. Which basically meant I couldn't freeze anything
for a month because there was no room.

Anyway, disaster strikes one day, midweek, on my own. The
switches in our kitchen are very confusing; basically you can
only have a certain number of things on at any one time
otherwise everyone dies, or something, so for the extractor
fan to come on you have to flick off the dishwasher and so
on. OK? So. I accidentally turn the freezer off for about a
day. And when I open it, it's like a massacre, it's like
bleeding Viennettas everywhere, and it's just not worth the
grief I'd get from Chris so I go and replace them all; I
mean, the share price of Viennetta must have gone up that
day, I'm sure.

I do wonder sometimes, you know companies like that, like
Viennetta, which has pretty much Not Changed for a
decade – you get your vanilla one, you get your mint, and
that's about it. The chief execs, at that company, when they
arrive every day at work, and have their morning meeting,
what do they do? Do they literally just kind of look at each
other and say (*shrugs*) 'What, keep making it? Yeah. More of
the same? OK. Cool. See you on the golf course'. Boggles
my mind, honestly.⟩

'The Office – Series Two' DVD – 23 October 2009

Ben   I know what this was. Yeah, look, St Pancras.
Something to watch on my laptop, cheer me up on the train
to see Josh. This was . . . I dunno, maybe three months after
his accident down here. So . . .

I got a train up on the Friday night which I hated
because I hadn't booked in advance so I didn't get a

seat and everyone was off home for the weekend so
I had to stand, so I couldn't watch the DVD anyway. And I
was rammed in the buffet car, which didn't open, because
the train was too full, and I wanted a drink, which I don't
think was unreasonable given I was on my way to see my
brother . . . you know. And I couldn't even have a little
drink, and I remember being disproportionately angry
about that.

Had the most ginormous lump in my throat as I walked
down the corridor to the ward, just waiting for that moment
when I'd see my mum and dad's faces, and they would both
probably first do that 'smile bravely, happy to see you' thing,
and then do that 'face slowly crinkle', erm, thing, and I'd
have to try and not cry so that they wouldn't but just the
thought of it was enough to make my bottom lip tremble in
that way that it does.

Josh was in his bed. It was dark by then. Jonathan Ross was
on the telly.

Friday nights in hospitals are strange. It doesn't feel like
anyone is going to die.

He smiled when I walked in. Said 'hey'. But he couldn't
move, hardly at all. By then. His immune system was very
weak. There had been . . . complications. He looked . . . a
different shape. There were wires.

The last image I have of him as I walked out of the ward
was him going 'wait, wait, watch'. And he managed to creak
his thumb up. Just a bit. Which made him laugh. And made
me . . .

Drinks. Toucan pub – 17 September 2009

Ben Do you know the Toucan pub on . . . (*looking*). What
street? It's just off Soho Square. I didn't, but it's famous for
Guinness apparently, and I was a little surprised when she –
Amy; Oyster Card Girl, met on the tube – when she asked
for a pint of Guinness and I was like . . . well, I actually
think I laughed, which probably isn't . . . on a first date, you

ask someone their drink and then laugh in their face like they're an idiot, but I genuinely thought she was joking, she's like this tiny . . . . I doubted she could even hold the glass. Oh God, this is all coming out like I'm some patronising, misogynistic . . . misogynist, but . . .

I remember having Not Remembered how red her hair was, either, when . . . I'm not saying that, like . . . as in I've got anything – in fact I don't, the opposite, you know the one from Girls Aloud, ginger, I must the only guy in the world who'd actually quite – anyway. Maybe it's because on Facebook it had seemed darker in her photos. I'd scrawled through them, obviously – don't look at me like that, we all do it, you just do, don't you.

I wasn't sure it was a date at the time, in fact I'm still not. We'd been messaging each other online and, without blowing my own . . . you know, thing, I think I can occasionally be a little bit funny and charming online, because there's no eye contact needed and there's also a delete button. My God I wish I had a delete button in normal life.

You're all probably wishing I did as well.

So this was actually just a drink, a casual drink, after work. Well it was casual for her, she just worked around the corner at this, erm, PR, company, place, but, for me it was actually a bit of a schlep, but I still tried to act like I was swinging by. Not like I'd made an effort. Which I had.

I won a bit of money on the *Trivial Pursuit* machine, which I think impressed her a bit because I answered a question about Tolstoy but to balance it out I also got one right about Wayne Rooney, just so she didn't think I was a total . . .

So she didn't think I was me.

She has this brilliant attitude towards everything which I like; which I envy. Just everything is quite amusing or funny to her. She does this look constantly, especially when I bullshit about something which she won't let me get away with.

Like this.

(*Does it.*)

Not in a 'you're a dick head' kind of way. Just a kind of . . . sweet way.

And there was obviously something about her that made me feel comfortable because I acted fine all night. I would have actually been quite happy to sit and talk to me, that night. Which is very rarely the case.

She went her way, I went mine, with phone numbers this time. When's a long enough waiting time before you text? (Never get that right.) That night, morning after, weekend? Dunno. Anyway, we'd stayed out too late and I'd missed the last tube which meant it was a night bus from Trafalgar Square but for the first time ever on a night bus I didn't mind. In fact I think for the first time ever in the history of anyone on night buses anywhere, I was smiling . . .

Caffè Nero's – any date

Ben Right, brilliant, I'm going to ask Lisa about these, because sometimes – does anyone here work from home? Do you know sometimes you literally can't stay and work in the house anymore and you have to get out, well sometimes the best place to go to is a café and work and you have to buy something if you're going to sit there so, you know, surely that's . . . maybe.

Actually, can I tell you something? I'm a little bit proud of this, even though it was a little bit cheeky, but it's the one and only time I ever stood up against like a corporation or anything, ever. So amongst all these receipts, I kept noticing loads of Caffè Nero ones and you know how they give you that card to stamp? And when you get ten stamps you get a free coffee. Well this one time, at the one on The Cut near

Waterloo, I didn't have my card, so the girl there, quite
pretty actually, she said just keep the receipt and we'll stamp
it next time you're in. And it was like a (*angel-like noise*)
'aaarrhhh', like a ray of light moment, and so I said, can I
do that with any receipts I've saved, and she said 'yeah', and
so I thought 'right'. And I went back the next day with a
shoe box of about what I think was nearly sixty-four receipts
over a period of a year and a half (I drink a lot of coffee),
and they argued and cursed a bit but I stood my ground
and they gave in and not only *that* but they got so sick of
counting them they just gave me a handful of stamped
cards and told me to go away. I've still got some left. And
sometimes I've felt guilty about that, especially as I'm
normally so straight down the line about everything, but it
wasn't actually breaking the rules, and I think getting some
free coffees from a big corporate chain isn't quite the same
as swindling public services out of less tax. In my head. But
my head can be quite strange sometimes.

Inland Revenue   There's a level of allowance you're allowed
when working away from home, but it has to be within
reason.

Ben   What's within reason?

Inland Revenue   Well it depends on how much you've
earned. Best advice I can give is just not to take the piss.

Ben   Is that the official treasury line?

Inland Revenue   No, that's mine.

Ben   Oh OK. Do you like coffee? What's your favourite?

Inland Revenue   Cappuccino, normally. Boring, I know.

Ben   I've never understood cappuccinos, aren't they just
lattes with less in them. Lattes with half of it foam.

Inland Revenue   I like the foam bit.

Ben   Do you ever buy any muffins or anything? I try not to
but –

Inland Revenue   No, I'm very good like that. Just a bottle of sparkling water now and again.

Ben   Sparkling?! Oh my God, I don't think I can do this with you, we're too different.

Inland Revenue (*laughing*)   What?

Ben   Cannot stand sparkling, I have a real problem with it. Why is it fizzy? As a general rule, I think, if it doesn't have any taste, it shouldn't fizz. It, it's not right. I have very strong opinions on this.

Inland Revenue   Right, well, I'm not changing I'm afraid, so . . .

Ben   Would you like a coffee, I've got loads of stamped cards; I can post one up if you like. Then it'll be like I'm taking you out for a coffee. As a . . . you know, thank you. Thing. Only you'll be drinking it all alone. And I'm not really paying for it, so, actually, it's a bit rubbish, but, you know.

Inland Revenue   Awh, are you sure? Erm. Yeah OK. That's very kind, Ben. Thank you.

Ben   You're welcome.

Cream tea, Park Lane Hotel – 26 September 2009

Ben   Oh right, OK. Yeah. (*Beat. Stares at the ticket for a bit.*)

Yeah. OK. This was nearly the whole family, actually, down for . . .

Josh felt bad that I was always coming up to Chesterfield to see him, and that he'd never once, even once, been down to London. So last summer they all organised a trip down. They wanted to get there and back in a day. For Josh. He was often relying on a wheelchair by now, but could still stand and walk a little. If he wanted.

Still cooler than me. One of those 'piss take' sense of humours. Can't open your mouth without him . . . you know . . . picking up on some . . .

But he wanted to use the day and do really, really 'London' things. And so cream tea was my idea, showing off, wanted them to think this was what I do every Saturday, huh. Now I'm 'a Londoner, yah'.

And then the Natural History Museum, too – does anyone . . . ? Are there like tickets for that? Someone's got? No? Oh, yeah, maybe that's because it's free to get in. Idiot. So yeah, that was where we went in the afternoon, National History Museum. Of course. It's what you do, isn't it.

The reason the fall happened was because . . .

The reason the fall happened was because we were in the Dinosaur gallery. They have lots of different models and actual fossils of . . . well, I'm sure you've all been. Maybe.

I think he was embarrassed about the wheelchair, perhaps because it was London. In Chesterfield he never gave a shit, but maybe something to do with . . . it being *this* city, he was a bit more self aware. Wanted to be on his feet as much as possible.

There are some steps leading from the gallery level down to the main hall where the big . . . is it a brontosaurus or something? The big famous one, anyway.

Massive.

We were waiting for the lift because we didn't want to take the stairs; the grand, stone steps they have. There was a member of staff there waiting for us. Josh was on his feet; he wanted to get the, like, the panoramic view of the dinosaur so I took his hand and we wandered to near the top of the steps but leaning on the, erm . . . (what do you) just like the rail thing. But stone. Whatever. To look out across the main hall. Mum and my uncle were talking to the guide. My uncle about the route they got down here on, and the route they were taking back. In the way men do.

I have literally no idea where they came from. The kids. I heard them before I saw them. Three girls. Probably about five or six. They were playing with plastic models of velociraptors.

We turned and had let go of the . . . balustrade? (Is that what's it's called?)

The girls had started to fight. Over the models.

They knocked into me first and I kind of . . . stumbled *into* Josh.

Which made him wobble.

It didn't look like it was going to be that bad at first, he wasn't even going down, just shuffling backwards. Trying to correct himself. And I had hold of him still but . . . not quite. It was awkward. And he went over on the first step and I went over with him. I put my hand out so I only slid down a few steps.

I was kind of facing up the stairs at this point so I didn't see it, but I heard the crack because it was really loud and almost seemed to echo around that big, old hall.

It was his knee, the first break. We later found out.

The way he gathered speed as he rolled down those steps . . .

There's a part of me still which almost wants to . . .
to . . . laugh – it's OK, I know it's just that nervousness, you're allowed to . . . smile, I know what it's like.
The image of someone . . . falling, I know it's . . . it all seems a little . . .

But it was . . . I'd . . . it's definitely the most, erm, yeah, horrific thing I've ever seen happen to someone I . . .
(love) . . .

He was conscious. His eyes were blinking when I reached him. He hadn't fallen all the way; he'd stopped half way down. He was looking at me, and I knew he would be OK.

You know, immediately. He'd hurt himself. A lot. Would need a pot. Some crutches. For a while. But I suppose what I mean is . . . it was the look in his eyes, in both our eyes probably, that said . . . what will happen now? Because of his thing. His condition. Over the coming weeks, and months, how much extra . . . bone? Would grow? Now?

Too much?

He just looked. 'Resigned'. As he lay there. I was . . . .

. . . 'frustrated' doesn't quite seem the . . .

But just that we'd . . . used up most of his quota, I suppose. In one go.

As the paramedics attended to him I remember looking up at the neck and the head of the brontosaurus. The fossils, the skeleton that had caged something that had died centuries ago. Still here.

Oyster Card top-up – 21 August 2009

Ben   I know there's loads of, erm, Oyster Card top-up receipt things flying around but uh . . . this is gonna make me sound like a – but I know this one. Because I drew a little star on the back. Just so I'd remember. It was the first time I met Amy. Thursday . . . ? Yeah, Thursday morning. I like Thursday mornings. I think.

I was off to collect some books I ordered at this specialist shop place in Bloomsbury. The girl in front of me touched her card on the reader wrong, or too quickly, or something, so it beeped and the barrier didn't open, but as I was quick behind her, I put my Oyster Card on the reader, the barriers opened, and not knowing what to do, she walked through on my . . . you know, thing. So that when I touched in again, the barriers didn't open, it didn't work. And she turned round, and looked at me.

So she said 'oh, sorry'. In this . . . voice, and offered just to pass me her card over the barrier, because hers hadn't been read. And so she did, and I scanned hers, walked through the barrier, and gave it her back. Smiling, and saying thanks.

And then we heard the 'oy' from the guy in the booth thing, coming out and saying we can't do that, lend people our cards and things, and so I tried to explain, but I wasn't doing it very well, because it was very confrontational and I go all red in those situations and my throat dries. And he actually led us both into the office to take our cards and print out a reading thing to prove that we'd both got enough money and only touched in once each. Just on, you know, on the *other person's* card.

And I think because I hadn't been expecting to talk to a girl so I hadn't had a chance to get worked up, and because something a bit random had happened so I had a, I had a *subject matter* to talk about, I think is the reason why I did OK. And why by the time she got off the tube at Tottenham Court Road, she gave me her name to look up on Facebook. Which I did.

Les Misérables theatre ticket – 11 December 2009

Ben   This was when Mum was down, just before Christmas. Present shopping even though we all told her not to bother this year because of what had happened, family wise. But she said that would make her feel worse, if she didn't. Met her . . . yeah, in Covent Garden and she was being quite perky. We had a mulled wine. I remembered thinking that it was good. Remembered thinking why don't I drink this more; I'd drink it in spring if I could.

I'm not sure she liked the play – well, musical. Wasn't quite in the frame of . . .

She only picked to see it because of the Susan Boyle song, you know.

I don't care what people, critics, whoever, always say about everything on television being for the young now – tell you something, X Factor, Britain's Got Talent, Strictly Dancing

in the Jungle With a Celebrity or whatever; my mum and
her friends, in their forties and fifties, they are in absolute
heaven at the weekend, they bloody love it.

I heard this thing once, someone tell me if this is true, that
Ant and Dec, that they're insured on each other's life, like
for millions, in case the other one dies.

Because they need each other. Like . . . two halves of the
same whole.

Always stay on the same side of each other, don't they. Odd,
must be, but not, I suppose, after that length of time. Always
to look, to your left, for example, and always have that . . .
that other half of you there.

What's the thing, that other fact, about when you lose a limb
– phantom, that's it. A phantom . . . when you can still feel,
literally still *feel* it, even after it's . . .

(*Beat. Then lighter, but forced.*)

I'm talking about Ant and Dec, ahah. Sorry. Instead of . . .
(what?) – Mum! Christmas. There we go.

We got a bit too drunk, back at mine. That night. It was
strange just sat in my flat with just my mum, just having
some drinks. It opened her up a bit. Which meant she got
quite emotional. And then very emotional. And then pretty
hysterical, actually. And . . . and I was absolutely rubbish at
saying the right thing. Only I've never seen anyone so
completely and utterly broken before. So that's my excuse.

She talked about going to see someone. To talk to.
Professionally. My uncle's suggestion. I was surprised.
Always thought of all that as being a bit . . . middle class. Bit
southern. And she was the opposite, on both counts. From
where you just deal with it. Yourself. Anything else is just . . .
indulgence.

She wondered if I'd ever thought about it. And to my
surprise, I did. Half-heartedly.

Kept asking why I didn't come up to visit more, and I lied
and said work, and lied and said I would try to more and I
know all of this is so completely selfish; I should be going up
there, I should be *up* there, given that I could do my job
most places, but the thought of being there, of being in that
room, of living in the shadow of that crooked, fucking,
church spire all the time . . .

And so I don't. And I'm leaving them to get on with it
without me. Because down here I can forget. And I do know
that's awful, so you don't need to . . . look at me like . . .⟩

Sofa cushions, Debenhams – 28 April 2009

Ben   Oh. This was, erm . . . for Sam and Luke's wedding.
Civil partnership. Off one of those gift lists they send out. It
was in Worcester, the ceremony. They're Rachel's – my, erm,
ex – they're her friends really, but I got to know them quite
well. Especially Luke, he was a teacher too. Not the best day.
We'd already had our little chat about . . . not being, erm,
being certain about what we were doing. Nothing like going
to a wedding when you're in doubt about your own, uh . . .
about where *you* are going. I don't mean to the wedding, we
both knew we were going to Worcester. Even though I
actually didn't know where Worcester was, I thought it was
in like Devon. But anyway . . .

First gay wedding I'd been to. It was pretty cool. Really
cool, actually.

Lady Gaga, if you're interested, the first dance. Hardly a
slow, rocking from side to side ballad, but there you go.
Reminded me of my mum and dad. Actually.

Not because I was there for their first dance, obviously not,
I mean it just reminded me of them. My dad hates any kind
of . . . public display of . . . and, as 'the legend' goes – and
by that I mean my mum and her sisters every time they get
together – he could only stand being up there on the dance

floor with my mum for about thirty seconds and then had to duck out. 'A Whiter Shade of Pale'.

That was probably already the beginning of the end. For them two. If you plotted things back. It probably started there.

I got very drunk. Must have been lying on the grass outside the tent at some point. Had mud stains on my knees. I was probably being sick.

Streetvan – 5 June 2009

Ben   Oh yeah. Moving house. Flat. Slightly depressing, not gonna lie. I loved my old house. Cavendish Road.

June, yeah, so my 'business' wasn't a business properly by this point, and we were still, like, half a year until Granddad's money came through so it was a case of accepting I couldn't afford to live on my own, after Sal and Casey and her Dick Head boyfriend had moved out, so . . .

First moved down here, London I mean, in God, well, four, five years ago, whenever that was. Found myself in Tooting, don't know why, but a lot of people seem to, somehow. Should be something on the sign, Tooting, as you arrive. Like . . .

'Sorry. But, let's all just try and make the best of it, yeah?'

So, but, every year since then, though, literally once a year, I've moved one stop further up the Line, as my circumstances improved. First from Tooting Broadway to Tooting Bec, then Balham, then Clapham South, where I was last year. I calculated that, all being well, at that rate, I'd have a riverside apartment by 2016.

But as circumstances changed, back I go – yeah, actually, like snakes and ladders, I'm on a snake now see, back to Balham. I'm like some sort of economic barometer all on my own, actually, me. Sod the FTSE 100, just look how high or low I am on the Northern Line to test the economic strength of the what's-it. Country. 'And today in the markets, Ben dropped three stops down to Colliers Wood'.

Morden almost certainly representing some kind of worldwide financial collapse. End of the line? Too bloody right, have you been? Jesus.

So yeah, now, at this rate, I'm gonna have to wait for global warming to bring the river to *my* apartment, huh. Actually no, shouldn't joke, environmental issues; don't really want South London to become submerged under water, obviously.

Maybe Elephant and Castle.

I'm being slightly optimistic when I say I'm back in 'Balham', though, if I'm honest; Elmbourne Road is more Tooting Bec. Nice location to be fair, right on the Common. And I can *see* Balham from where I am, so, technically . . .

Balham's one of those places that's labelled as 'up and coming'. Permanently, as far as I can tell. I was in its 'library' once when –

– sorry, why did I use air quotes then? Like it's some *hypothetical* book depository; what a git, it's perfectly nice, a perfectly good . . . (*tuts*). Such a snob sometimes, hate that about . . .

Anyway, it's a perfectly good 'library' – oh my God, see, can't stop doing it now, fuck it – 'library', I was in, one time, saw an old magazine from like the mid eighties, and even back then it labelled Balham as 'up and coming', so I'm guessing it's just one of those places which is always coming but never actually comes.

There's an innuendo there somehow, but that's not really me, I'd blush, so have a moment just to make up your own, maybe. It'd be funnier than mine anyway.

Suit from Marks and Spencers – 4 April 2009

Ben Yeah, that's my new suit. I suppose I could put that in expenses, I did have it in my head somewhere that I needed a good suit for work, if I was going to be self employed. Never had to wear it for work though – why would I?

Rachel insisted on coming because she knew I'd settle for one that didn't fit. On the cusp of breaking up, but not quite. So that was. Fun.

Went for charcoal because you can wear it to weddings and funerals and everything then, can't you?

As I stood looking at myself in the dressing room mirror, the thought entered my head that the first time I wore it for anything might actually be for his funeral.

My . . .

No accidents had happened yet or anything but you just now when something isn't far away, don't you, and . . .

I knew there was Sam and Luke's wedding in a fortnight, of course, but I guess another part of me thought I wouldn't be going. That in the few days Rachel and I would . . . I don't know.

I am gonna put that in expenses, you know, because I do often wear a suit on my videos. So there. (*Drops it into the 'Expenses' box.*)

Thing is, I don't mind paying tax, incidentally. I'm actually one of those annoying people who believe that you shouldn't swindle or try to pay less. Maybe it was growing up in the north (well, kind of). Tony Benn was MP for Chesterfield, you know.

Romans, it was the Romans who began the idea of taxation in this country, though I think the Egyptians did something similar before that – see, this is like one of my lessons. They're normally more interesting than this, I have music and stories. Visual aids.

Pretty much the first well known story about tax in this country is Lady Godiva, whose husband promised to reduce the levies in Coventry if she promised to ride through the town naked.

Now. I've been to Coventry, on a Saturday night as it goes, someone's birthday, and a lady with no top on wouldn't raise many eyebrows anymore. I can tell you.

Little joke, there.

Seems like we're at a bit of a junction again, doesn't it? In the long history of 'tax'. This country. That's why I like history, it gives you 'the long view'.

I don't know. Just seems like after decades of flipping between one idea and another – one election, Labour, collectivism, chucking in more; next one, Conservative, individualism, chucking in less . . . I guess I naïvely thought that we'd reached a kind of national consensus. But now it seems like we're split again, 50/50, and suddenly we're not just arguing about tax, it's kind of . . . it's like what we're actually arguing about is literally 'what do we believe in'. What are our Principals? Our ideology, for the way we're going to live. And tax is just the . . . 'the case in point'.

I don't know. I see both sides, probably because of my family. Dad and Granddad, God, couldn't be more different. Maybe it's just that generation thing. Granddad of the war mindset, Atlee and all that, everything nationalised, 'we're in this together', kind of thinking. Lifelong member of the cooperative group. Dad a child of the sixties, I suppose, wanting to keep more money for himself. Secret Tory, though he'd never admit it.

But I see it, of course, I see how low tax can help; help businesses, people, grow and become strong that way, and I *should* be looking to pay less and fuck 'em (sorry).

But equally, I sometimes wonder whether or not we'd all be happier if we just spent less on drink and clothes and iPods and more on schools and hospitals and police. But I don't imagine everyone my age shares that view.

'The Man'. That's what he's called, isn't he. The tax man. You 'stick it to The Man'. Or 'The Man' comes after you. Course, the only contact with 'The Man' I have is Lisa.

And she doesn't sound all that scary. Actually.

Bottle of port – 14 October 2009

Ben   Oh my God. OK. Erm. Huh, this one makes me smile, actually. Which is odd because it's kind of about my Granddad. When he was dying, he decided to rejig his thing, his Will. We didn't know this at the time. He was quite old school and, for whatever reason, he decided that Josh and I wouldn't get our inheritance until we were older, more mature, when we needed it more, or something. We're not talking estates and heirlooms, but . . . 'some'.

I have my own theory. About Josh. My granddad giving him something to . . . aim for. Maybe. But . . .

Anyway, he did it for ten years after the date he changed it, making us twenty-seven. Died about a month or so after. So we should have got it in October 08, which was . . . (*sigh*), this makes me sound like a . . . but that was one of the reasons I thought I could quit my job and start the website business. With this capital. Anyway, turns out no, some legal mumbo jumbo, the difference between 'in the tenth year' and 'in ten years' or something meant apparently it wasn't until *last* October, 09, despite the fact I'd handed my notice in at the council the year before. Hence why I was, erm . . . a bit poorer than I had thought I was going to be. Serves me right. Relying on 'inherited wealth'. Everything my granddad was against. Maybe that's why he did it.

It took me a while to understand why there was so much. When I got the cheque. Wondered why it was . . . double. What he'd said it would be.

And then I remembered.

It was Graham's vintage port, one of his favourites. So I had a little glass in his honour, the day it came in. To say thanks. His life spent working.

Nice, too.

Return train ticket London to Chesterfield – 31 October 2009

Ben Oh, this was erm . . . funeral. Back home.

I know people always say there were loads of people there but there were loads of people there. My granddad's funeral was . . . not really very full. Tragic, I suppose really, the longer you live, the less people are around to come to your funeral. Josh was only twenty-seven, so . . . I guess those are often quite well attended.

Close to the entrance of the . . . I'm sorry, I'm literally no good with, erm . . . 'ecclesiastical' terminology – apart from that – chapel, church? Chapel? Close to the way in, anyway, is the children's part of the cemetery, and you can tell what it is because it's so colourful. They have toys and balloons and . . . I think they put it there to try and get you going before you walk in, deliberately. Like the opposite to a warm up act before a show, but the same principal. Loosen you up. Remember while I was waiting to go in, this man was draping a blue Chelsea top over a little headstone in there.

Mum and Dad have never said that they . . . held any . . . towards me. About the accident that happened. Which doesn't mean that I don't but . . .

I guess it's just the idea of coming from the exact same egg. But being given two completely different chances in life. And one of us made the absolute most of the *lack of chance* he had. And the other has been wasting the amount he's been given.

I thought I would be a mess but I think I only cry when other people cry and for whatever reason, Mum next to me was being really . . .

I could hear people behind me blubbering from the word go – and that's fine. Of course that's fine. I think sometimes, though, it's the occasion, the idea, that actually makes people sad. Like watching a sad film. You're not *really*

heartbroken at a film, are you? You don't . . . *feel* it. You're
not . . . 'grieving'.

I only nearly went when the Jacko song came on, when
the curtain closed around the . . . (coffin) . . . and
I'd remembered hearing it being talked about before
but it was only when it actually came on did I think
it was a bad idea. Because it made it all about me.
Because it was my name. The song. And I hated that
because then I felt it looked like I was trying to steal
the . . . or something.

I didn't like the way people were looking judgementally at
Dad. For leaving. Earlier in the year. It had been mutual,
him and Mum. Josh had said it was all right, more than
that, he'd practically bloody asked them to . . . because he
knew they'd been staying together for him. Just waiting for
him to . . .

Maybe I was imagining it, maybe no one was looking. He
didn't stay for the thing after though. I watched him walk
off towards his car. So slowly. His hands in his trouser
pockets.

I have *tried* to like that song . . . tried. Always. When Josh
would sing it at me, jokily, sometimes deliberately trying to
wind me up. But I just, I can't. So sentimental. So . . .

I don't know.

I just kept my head down, staring at my trousers. There was
still that mud stain showing, despite the fact I got my suit
dry cleaned. Couldn't remember where that had come
from . . .

Up cinema ticket – 12 October 2009

Ben   Went to the IMAX to watch this with Amy. Oyster
Card girl. Technically I suppose it was our first date because
I've no idea whether the drinks in Soho was a date or just
a . . . a pre-date. Anyway, I can't say date without cringing,
it's so . . . *High School Musical*.

And I didn't want to come across like a complete, socially inept prude. So I remember deciding to inch my hand over hers at some point during the film. Which meant I couldn't enjoy the first hour and a half of the film. Unluckily I'd finally plucked up the courage to do it at the moment something 3D flew out of the screen. So Amy put her hand to her mouth in shock just as I . . . (*Demonstrates*.)

So then I kind of had to pretend I'd gone a very long way round to do the same.

Which she didn't buy because she turned and smiled at me, and she took hold of my hand and put it on her lap so that was fine.

They're expensive, aren't they? Relationships. You 'do' things. Meals. Films. Plays. Peddle boats. Mind you, Amy insists on paying half of everything, not like Rachel, I'd pay for the meals then – odd, isn't it? Still. Or maybe not. Dunno. She'd happily let me pay the bill but had a go that time I held the door open for her. So there you are, I obviously don't know the rules. Maybe no one does.

She joked towards the end that I had more moisturising creams and face washes and stuff than she had. I didn't want to get them, they were bought for me, and every other guy I knew had started . . . you know.

They want you to still be a 'bloke' bloke a lot of the time, but also have feelings and nice skin. It's a fine line, and I'm not sure I'm treading it. I dunno.

I took Amy out for our first meal though – does anyone have it? It was Bluebird, on Kings Road. No?

Paid for that. It felt right, doing that. As The Man. I know, how 'un-modern', but . . . I dunno. Deep down I still think it's expected. Wanted. Almost. By both sides. Some of the old ways. Simpler ways.

I dunno.

That bus journey back to my house that night – not this one, the Bluebird one. The 319 through Clapham Junction, that was . . . that was bad. Top deck (why did we sit on the top deck? Idiot.) Some lads behind us making comments about Amy.

What they'd like to do to her.

I was completely and utterly paralysed, I did nothing. She would have stopped me from saying or doing anything I'm sure, because I would have probably died, but the fact is I didn't say or do anything, I just did nothing, because I didn't know what to do.

We never spoke about it after. But I think I must have disappointed her. In a way.

That was maybe going to be the first time we . . . you know. Properly 'spent' the night together.

We just went to sleep instead.

This exchange between **Ben** *and the* **Inland Revenue** *should be added in by the actor at a convenient point around halfway through the play.*

Ben   Lisa, I've got receipts which are, erm, dated from before the actual tax year starts in April, but if they're business expenses can I still –

Inland Revenue   Yes, you are allowed a certain amount of set-up costs which can be spread forward to this year. So. Anything else? How's it all going, all right?

Ben   Erm. Erm. Yeah. I guess, it . . . it's going. So.

Inland Revenue   Well, I don't envy you.

Ben   Have you ever had to do one?

Inland Revenue   No, never. Ironically enough. Always been PAYE for me.

Ben   Have you always worked at the Inland Revenue?

Inland Revenue   No. Although it feels like it. It's a good job, though, nice people. Close to where I live.

Ben Do you like Wrexham?

Inland Revenue I don't dislike it. All my family are here. It's not quite London, but . . .

Ben Huh. Well. London's not quite London. In a way.

Inland Revenue How do you mean?

Ben I don't know. I mean. I don't know. The idea of what living here is like is . . . it's different to . . . I mean it's amazing now, when I speak to family, or friends back home, the mere mention of living in London still provokes this . . . 'ooh, London ey? Wow, look at you.'

I can't do anything now, like put a sugar in my tea or check my phone without Mum going, 'Ooh you and your London ways'. I think she thinks I spend every evening at launch parties and galas or something.

Inland Revenue (*laughs*) Awh, she's probably just proud of you.

Ben (*beat*) All I knew of London was Richard Curtis films and Bridget Jones. I had visions of what it'd be like before I came here. To study. Walking over the Thames to get to work in the morning, didn't matter where I worked, I assumed you had to walk over the Thames to get there. Evening drinks in wine bars with my friends, surrounded by the city lights, bemoaning our current 'relationships', providing support, hailing cabs, dashing to meet other friends at the theatre, going to the opening nights of exhibitions, somehow, didn't matter, just assumed somehow I would. Saturday afternoons having picnics in Royal Parks and Sunday afternoons reading a classic novel in a little café by the river.

But I don't. I don't make lots of cool meals that I find in newspapers and magazines. I don't have a fully stocked pantry of ingredients that I picked up from the market at the weekend, I just stop by Sainsbury's, every night, and buy 'a meal', and eat that meal, that night, in front of the telly. And if I go out with friends it's the same old pubs that we know and I've never even been to a couple of the parks, ever, and if I do read a book it's on the tube and that's only if I'm awake enough not to fall asleep.

Because I guess somewhere none of us think of this as being our life, this is just a gap, a temporary delay in the service, before we start properly. Or something. But then suddenly you realise that it has started. And this is it.

(*Looking at his receipt.*) If these are it. If this is everything I've experienced and done for a year.

Then . . .

Inland Revenue   . . . Ben?

More iTunes receipts

Lion King Soundtrack – 'I Just Can't Wait To Be King'

Ben   OK, again, don't judge, this is another teaching chess soundtrack, online. For the King obviously. 'Everywhere you look I'm standing in the spotlight'. Yeah? No?

Rowan Atkinson.

I think I kind of associate with, erm, the King. On the chess board. Which probably sounds quite narcissistic. But it's, actually, when you think about it, he's like one of the weakest . . . you know, and he has everyone huddled around him, to protect him. Because they're all willing to sacrifice for him, because they're strong and they can swoosh around, and all he can do is, is move . . . you know, one little step. At a time.

Les Misérables (Original Soundtrack) – 'I Dreamed A Dream'

Ben   Oh. *Les Mis*. It's the one Mum likes, so I got it for her.

Michael Jackson – 'Ben'

Ben *just stands and listens to this one for a while . . .*

Procol Harum – 'A Whiter Shade Of Pale'

Ben *just stands and listens to this one for a while . . .*

The Tango Project – 'Por Una Cabeza'

Ben   Oh. I got this in preparation. For my dance class.
Basically you do this like induction thing over the first
month where Rea at the Leisure Centre place introduces
you to all the dances she can do, like jive and, erm . . .
ballroom and lots of others. And then from then on you
pick one and specialise.

I wasn't really finding, erm . . . none of them really
grabbed me.

I was doing it to get over it. To get over that fear of . . .
having spent virtually all of my childhood not running or
not jumping and certainly not dancing for fear of . . .

But then Rea started showing me this, erm . . . well, they're
called 'non-contact' dances, all from like the fifties and
sixties, things like the twist and what have you, where you
don't have to touch anyone or bounce into anyone and
there's no risk of, erm . . .

(*Deep breath.*) So. Erm. I'm happy to, uh . . . you know. In
the spirit of – I'm happy to maybe show you a couple. If
you'd like. Or not. I don't mind.

Yes? Erm. OK. Well.

Turns 'Por Una Cabeza' *off and replaces it with The Water Boys*
'The Whole of The Moon'.

Something more upbeat. OK. Just a couple. This . . . is the
Hitch Hike. (*Demonstrates.*)

Thumb up, one-two-three to the side, like that. Yes?

Erm. This is the Pony. (*Demonstrates.*)

Jump to the right, this foot, jump to the left, up, and so on.

And erm . . . OK, this is Watusi. (*Demonstrates.*) All in the hips.
There. That's it. Done.

This exchange between **Ben** *and the* **Inland Revenue** *should be
added in by the actor at a convenient point close to the end of
the play when nearly all receipts have been taken from the
audience.*

Ben   Oh, hello, sorry, I, I asked to be put through to Lisa.

Inland Revenue   Ah, I'm afraid Lisa's not around today,
can I help at all?

Ben   Not around? What do you mean, not at work? What's
the problem?

Inland Revenue   Is this a personal call, sorry?

Ben   No, I just, I want to know where she is, what's wrong
with her.

Inland Revenue   I think she just called in sick. I can pass
on a message, if that's – ?

Ben   No, I . . . it – I wanted to ask her about dance classes.

Inland Revenue   Dance classes?

Ben   I'm taking dance classes.

Inland Revenue (*pause*)   Right.

Ben   I want to know if I should put the dance classes in as
expenses, because even though I'm using them a little bit
for personal reasons I think they might also be useful for
my online video things.

Inland Revenue   Well I'd need to know a little bit more
about the nature of your business if I were to / advise on –

Ben   Lisa knows the nature of my business, I don't
understand. What's – how . . . when will she be back?

Inland Revenue   Well I don't think we're expecting her in
for the rest of the week.

Ben   For the re – . . . a whole week?! (*Tries to calm down*.)

Can I have her home number please? I'm not weird, I promise.

Inland Revenue   Sir, any enquiries you have, I will be able to help with.

Ben   No, I can't talk to you!

Inland Revenue   Why not?

Ben   Because you're not her . . .

Inland Revenue   Sorry – ?

Ben   Because you're not – !!

I will leave a message, can you get her to call me when she's back.

Inland Revenue   Of course, what's your number?

Ben   She has it.

Inland Revenue   And your name.

Ben   Ben.

Inland Revenue   Ben what?

Ben   She'll know. She'll . . .

Inland Revenue   I'm sorry, but we do have a lot of people calling –

Ben   She'll know, all right?! Fuck. She'll . . . k – . . . she'll know.

Teddy Bear, Hamleys – 14 February 2010

Ben   This was when Casey had her baby. Jack (great name). Casey who I lived with on Cavendish Road. Her, me, and Salim. We'd all done our PGCE together. Sal was the first to go, he fell in love, in fact the story of that house is basically people falling in love and leaving, one by one, until it was just me, haha. Erm. Yeah, Sal went to his girlfriend's, now wife, so Casey moved The Dick Head in with us, made worse by him being around so much. About a year or so ago he found a black hair in a Ferrero Rocher and this somehow got him a lot of money and so he just mooched around the house all day, pissing me off. And then eventually they moved out together.

Bit of a wake up call. Going to Casey's. Very strange and . . . yeah, slightly disconcerting, seeing people you grew up with, studied with, the same age as you, all starting to reproduce. Sal was there with his baby girl, too. She was like walking and talking and everything. I'd seen her a year ago, she could barely hold up her head, now she's learnt a whole new language and motor skills. All in one year. What have . . . what have I done in that . . .

Never held a baby before. Casey held it out to me and I nearly picked it up by the head, like that, one hand; I mean what do you do, where do you learn that?

Where's the helpline for that? For all these . . . for becoming a . . .

Studio 6 restaurant – 17 December 2009

Ben   Oh yeah. I don't know if you know it, little place on the Southbank. Quite nice.

I knew what she was going to say. Amy. Oyster Card Girl. I'd been such a . . . an absolute miserable . . . erm, what am I trying to say – I knew what I was doing to her. Taking it out on her, everything that was happening at home. You have to be brave in front of colleagues and associates and friends don't you, but you can be as big a wreck as you want in front of your girlfriend. And so . . . I was.

She hadn't been able to get to the funeral; maybe that was it. She had a work thing, a launch thing, in . . . . Oh I don't – somewhere in Germany. Hamburg, maybe. And even though I pretended that was fine, I held it against her for the rest of our . . . erm, our time. I think.

She basically couldn't carry on the way things were. But at the time I was still so upset and angry and didn't really intend to change that any time soon, so . . .

Took a walk along the Southbank. Which was nice. I remember it being quite chilly – what month was it again?

As we started getting closer to London Bridge tube, I started to get a real sense of time running out, to change her mind, or add in a caveat to our agreement that meant if I did change, get better, happier, maybe we could see where we were, maybe after Christmas. She smiled, and said maybe, but I knew that meant no. I gave it a fortnight before she started to notice the looks and the glances of other boys, the ones she hadn't been looking for when she was with me.

I will miss her. I will miss how she wouldn't laugh for a while and then explode with laughter all in one go, like the time my phone rang and I answered the TV remote. I'll even miss how irrationally angry she could get, like at not being able to light her lighter, or not being able to fold newspapers, like the time she got so mad at *The Sunday Times* she went outside into the garden and set it on fire.

I'm so stupid.

I'm so stupid, why can't I keep hold of the things that make me . . . fucking . . . smile?

Inland Revenue   Hello, Lisa speaking.

Ben   Where were you yesterday?

Inland Revenue   Ben?

Ben   You weren't there, where were you?

Inland Revenue   I was off ill.

Ben   What was wrong with you?

Inland Revenue   Ben, I don't think that's / fair –

Ben   I needed you.

Inland Revenue   What for?

Ben   Dance lessons.

Inland Revenue   What?

Ben   Dance lessons, I want to know whether I should put down my dance lessons.

Inland Revenue   Oh. Sorry. I thought you were asking me to come to dance lessons.

Ben   . . . but you live in Wrexham.

Inland Revenue   Yes, I know that. What are the dance lessons for?

Ben   . . . I thought I might incorporate some dance into the videos.

Inland Revenue   Sounds like a good idea.

Ben   But I think that might be a bit of a lie, so I just wanted to check. I think I might just be wanting to do them because I've never really danced before. Because as a child I thought I might hurt myself if I did. But then when I realised I wouldn't hurt myself I still didn't do it. Even though Josh did; he danced all the time and sometimes he'd ask me to dance, in our room, just run around dancing to Michael Jackson and I never would, no matter how often he asked me, I never would. How stupid is that?

Inland Revenue   I don't think that sounds stupid.

Ben   I mean what kind of arsehole, am I? Too afraid to dance with my own brother.

I don't think I can do this. Every year.

Inland Revenue   What do you mean?

Ben   I don't think I can have this, this reliving thing, this 'marker', every year. That can't be a way to live your life, to be forced, every twelve months, to look back at all the things you did wrong, at all the people you did bad things to. I think I'll just end up never leaving the house to avoid doing anything that will make me sad when it comes to this.

I don't want to be sad any more, Lisa. I'd rather just give you too much money. And not have to do this.

Inland Revenue   Ben, that would be a first.

Ben   . . . huh. (*Smiles a little.*) It won't even be that much. I only earned about six.

Inland Revenue   Six? Six what?

Ben   Grand. Thousand.

Inland Revenue   You only earned six grand last year?

Ben   Yeah, all right.

Inland Revenue   No I'm not saying it because . . . I'm saying you have a six and half thousand pound allowance.

Ben   What's that?

Inland Revenue   When you're self employed you're allowed to earn up to £6,500 before we start taxing you.

Ben   . . . Six and a ha – . . . so I don't need to pay any tax?

Inland Revenue   Not this year, no.

Ben (*beat*)   So this whole thing has been a complete waste of time?!

Inland Revenue   I don't know. What do you think?

Ben *thinks*.

Inland Revenue   How did you live on six grand for a year?

Ben   My . . . I had some, erm . . . inheritance. That I . . . And my mum and dad, they erm . . .

Inland Revenue   Wow. You owe them a big thank you.

Ben   Yeah.

Yeah, I guess I should go and. See them.

Inland Revenue   Well. Anyway. It was nice to chat to you these past weeks. For what it was worth.

Ben   Thank you.

Inland Revenue   Maybe you should think about getting an accountant next year. Then you won't have to go through all this again, will you?

Ben (*beat*)   No, I think . . . I think maybe I'll, I'll keep, I'll do it, I'll give it another . . . it, it's probably – I think it's probably something I should. Erm. Do.

Inland Revenue   Well. If you're ever in the Wrexham area . . . could always pop in, ey.

Ben   Huh. Yeah. (*Beat.*) I never will be though.

Inland Revenue (*laughs*)   No. Why would you be? Keep up with your dance lessons, though, won't you?

Ben   Yeah. All right.

Music fades in.

Lights down.